Original title:
The Orange Orchard

Copyright © 2025 Creative Arts Management OÜ
All rights reserved.

Author: Vivienne Beaumont
ISBN HARDBACK: 978-1-80586-337-3
ISBN PAPERBACK: 978-1-80586-809-5

Fruity Reflections at Dusk

In the grove where the citrus grows,
A squirrel sings to the thorny rose,
He juggles fruits, a classy act,
But drops a lemon, oh! That's a fact.

The birds all cheer, they snap and caw,
As he mops up with a leafy straw,
A citrus twist upon his head,
Who knew that limes could dress a thread?

The trees are buzzing, all aflutter,
With gossip's zing and juicy clutter,
A dizzy bee in shades of zest,
Claims oranges wear the brightest vest.

As twilight dances, shadows blend,
A comedy of fruit, nature's friend,
So raise a glass to the grove's delight,
Where laughter ripens in evening light.

Echoes of Time in the Citrus Shade

In the grove where laughter blooms,
Orange blooms and tiny grooms.
Squirrels dance with zestful cheer,
Plucking fruit as joy draws near.

Hats askew and shoes untied,
Chasing sunshine, what a ride!
Lemonade spills on my face,
As citrus critters mock my grace.

Whispers of Hope among the Fruiting Trees

Twirling trees with branches wide,
Whispers sweet, and joy can't hide.
Bees in suits with tiny ties,
Buzzing laughter, oh what a surprise!

Dreams roll like oranges on the grass,
Tripping lightly as they pass.
In this grove, where silliness grows,
Even the shadows wear big bows.

The Charm of Sunkissed Days

Marmalade skies at break of dawn,
Chasing fruit 'til all are gone.
Jokes and giggles in the air,
Sun-kissed cheeks and hearty flair.

Tipsy trees sway to a tune,
Bouncing beats 'neath the afternoon.
Each sunset drips with golden light,
In this orchard, all feels right.

Sunset Citrus Serenade

As the sun sets, the glow is wild,
Lemonade parties, laughter styled.
Sipping tangy tales of glee,
Fruit-inspired poetry set free!

Orange skies, a peachy grace,
Dancing shadows, let's embrace!
Underneath the starry clues,
Citrus dreams, we can't refuse.

Sanguine Spheres of Delight

In a grove where laughter grows,
Spheres of zest put on a show.
In every bite, a giggle swells,
As sunlight twirls and softly yells.

The bees wear hats, the birds wear shoes,
Each fruit a prank, with silly hues.
Rolling down in playful jest,
Who knew juice could be the best?

Citrus Sunbeams on the Skin

Sunshine drips from every branch,
A sticky dance, a juicy chance.
Lemon drops and lime parade,
Mirthful moments, never fade.

Peels like socks all strewn about,
Oh what fun, let's twist and shout!
In this grove, we sing and spin,
With citrus joy, we wear the grin.

An Orchard's Embrace

A laughter hug from trees thus tall,
With fruity gifts, they give their all.
Citrus hugs are bright and bold,
In tangy tales, sweet dreams unfold.

We dance beneath the fragrant glow,
In patches where our giggles flow.
Each fruit a smile, each tree a friend,
In this joke book that won't end.

Twilight in the Citrus Fields

As twilight paints the skies with zest,
All the critters come for their fest.
Dancing shadows and peels that squeak,
In this twilight, joy hits its peak.

A fruit flew by, oh what a sight!
It tickled me with pure delight.
In the fading sun's embrace we stay,
With laughter light, we end the day.

Fruits Drenched in Golden Glimpse

In a grove where sunlight plays,
Orioles chatter, dance in rays.
Lemonade dreams and sticky feet,
Giggling kids can't be discreet.

Juicy secrets, sweet delight,
Mischief ripens in the light.
Fruits tumble, laughter flies,
In this orchard, joy always lies.

Sunkissed Lushness in the Grove

A squirrel steals the juiciest treat,
While bees buzz by, a lively beat.
Sun-kissed oranges roll and sway,
Chasing shadows, they seem to play.

Fruit fights happen, oh what fun!
Tangerines on the run!
Laughter fills the fragrant air,
In this grove, no worries care.

A Citrus Festival for the Soul

Zestful folks with grins so wide,
In fruit-filled carts, they all abide.
Juggling oranges is the norm,
As laughter bursts, a sunny storm.

Tartness tickles, sweetness twirls,
Frolicking in fruity swirls.
Every slice a joyous cheer,
Creating memories year by year.

Sundrenched Echoes in Shaded Valleys

Under trees, the shadows play,
Where giggling echoes dance away.
Citron croquet, it's a delight,
While ants parade, an eager sight.

A picnic spread, a fruit buffet,
Sticky fingers rule the day.
With orange slices, smiles expand,
Joyful moments, forever planned.

Blossoms of Daydreams

In a grove where dreams collide,
Fruits wear hats, oh what a ride!
Bunnies bouncing in the shade,
   Chasing shadows, unafraid.

A squirrel juggles with some zest,
While a bird sings, doing its best.
  The flowers giggle in the sun,
As bees compete in who's the fun.

Sweetness in the Breeze

There's a breeze that tells a tale,
Of sticky fingers—oh, I wail!
Lemonade dreams and sugar highs,
Under cotton candy skies.

Ants march by in a parade,
With tiny hats they've cleverly made.
A simple picnic turns to cheer,
When watermelon slice draws near.

Harvest Whispers of Flora

Amongst the greens, a secret's sown,
A cat who thinks it's all his own.
He's tasting fruits with suave delight,
While the veggies try to take flight.

The pumpkins laugh at how they roll,
Who knew a squash could be so whole?
In this patch, nonsense reigns supreme,
With playful antics like a dream.

Golden Groves at Dusk

As twilight wraps the grove's embrace,
Fireflies dance in a dazzling race.
A raccoon hides with a grin so wide,
In this orchard, mischief will abide.

Two ducks quack charts for a fun ride,
While owl disputes the time and tide.
In these golden hues of light,
The world is silly, the mood just right.

A Tapestry of Citrus and Sky

In a grove of bright delight,
Lemons gossip with the kite.
Tangerines try on a grin,
While oranges join in the din.

Branches sway in cheeky dance,
Wiggling fruit, they take a chance.
Laughing leaves, they share a joke,
As the sunbeams softly poke.

Memories in Each Ripened Sphere

Peeling back the skins of cheer,
A slice of life, that's crystal clear.
Sticky fingers, gleeful cries,
As sweetness takes us by surprise.

Buzzing bees wear tiny hats,
While squirrels hoard their tasty snacks.
Every fruit, a tale to tell,
In this fragrant citric well.

Sun-drenched Joy in Every Bite

With every bite, the sun does beam,
Juicy joy, a looped-up dream.
Sticky sap like candy rain,
As citrus jokes spill from the grain.

Pulped puns and zestful rhymes,
Echo through the swaying chimes.
In the midst of sour and sweet,
Laughter makes this day complete.

Conversations Held Between Branches

Branches stretch, they intertwine,
Swapping stories, oh so fine.
Fruit speaks loudly, skins ablaze,
In dappled light, they share their ways.

A citrus court, where jesters play,
While shadows bound in bright array.
Every chatter, bursts of cheer,
In this grove, there's naught to fear.

Sunkissed Adventures in Eden

In a grove where shadows play,
Lemons tell jokes to the day.
Limes roll laughter on the ground,
While orange giggles spin around.

Sunkissed glee in every bite,
Grapefruit dances, what a sight!
Bouncing sunbeams make us grin,
Witty fruits invite us in.

Nectar Trails of a Honeyed Dawn

Morning blooms with sticky cheer,
Buzzing bees, they hold us dear.
Peaches whisper sweet surprise,
Beneath the syrupy skies.

Honey drips on every tongue,
As citrus songs are gaily sung.
A taste of sunshine, what a treat,
With all the silly things to eat!

Fables of the Golden Fruits

Tales of fruit in storybooks,
Come alive with silly looks.
Bananas slip, they tend to slide,
While juicy tales we can't abide.

Peels that laugh, they dance about,
In this world, there's no doubt.
Golden wonders, what a spree,
Fables shared by fruity glee.

Citrus Chorus in the Sun

The sun is high, the chorus blooms,
Citrus voices chase away glooms.
Mandarins hum a joyful tune,
As zestful laughter fills the noon.

Lemons jive, with a twist and turn,
While elder fruits take time to learn.
In this bright and fruity throng,
The citrus sings its silly song.

The Sweetness of Airborne Tales

In the grove where giggles play,
A squirrel stole my snack today.
With twirls and flips, he dashed away,
While I just laughed and watched his sway.

The bees, they buzz with much delight,
Crashed into blooms, oh what a sight!
They dance around, all busy, bright,
And leave me swatting, what a fright!

Orchards Awash in Fluttered Wings

A butterfly took quite the stand,
On my nose, it licked my hand.
I sneezed and sent it off this land,
It whirled around like a tiny band.

The ladybugs on a leaf parade,
Counting spots in the sunlight's shade.
They jest and jive, yet I'm dismayed,
As I forgot the picnic I made.

A Canvas of Sunkissed Wonder

Above, a bird just sang a song,
It tried to woo a mate all wrong.
Two squirrels joined in, though not for long,
And plopped on branches, all day strong.

The sunbeams play a merry game,
While ants march by like soldiers tame.
I watch in awe, but feel some shame,
For here I sit—who's that to blame?

Golden Ripple of Tomorrow's Dawn

The morning light spills out like cheer,
While critters gather, drink their beer.
A crow drops nuts without a fear,
Proclaiming loudly, "This is my sphere!"

I trip on roots and roll with grace,
Attracting laughter from the space.
The trees all giggle in their place,
As I get up, a war-painted face!

Amber Echoes in Lush Canopies

In a grove where laughter grows,
Oranges giggle, strike a pose.
Squeezed with joy, they sing a tune,
Tap dance under the laughing moon.

Underneath boughs, we take a break,
Grappling with juice as we shake.
Fruitflies spin, the sun bounces,
Comedy blooms, as humor pounces.

Bees know jokes that leave us stunned,
Pollinating puns, they're so fun!
With every zest that we unleash,
Giggles in sunlight, pure caprice.

Citrus-Laden Heartstrings of Harmony

Peeling laughter, zestful glee,
Life's a drink, oh can't you see?
Bouncing bobs of yellow gold,
In this serenade, brave and bold.

Wobbling limbs of juicy delight,
Running around, what a silly sight!
Mixing flavors, laughter's cure,
Harmony in citrus—pure allure.

Every slice tells a tale so grand,
Like silly dances, hand in hand.
Sweet and tangy, joy does blend,
In our hearts, may fruit transcend.

Sunlight Fragments on Silvery Leaves

Sunbeams tickle the shimmering green,
A fruit parade, what a scene!
Silly shadows hop on by,
As branches jive and leaves comply.

Dewdrops glisten like goofy eyes,
As we share hugs and sweet goodbyes.
With every pitter-patter of feet,
We dance around, can't be beat.

Nature's chuckle fills the air,
Witty whispers of citrus flair.
Under these lights, we just can't stop,
Spinning like fruit, it's a wild hop!

Beneath the Citrus Canopy

Underneath this fruity roof,
Hang some jokes, let's make it goof!
Swinging limbs, a clumsy twist,
Citrus smiles that can't be missed.

Tickling vines with soft embrace,
Carrying laughter, a funny chase.
Oranges tumble, giggle, roll,
In this patch, we've found our soul.

Ripe with humor, sweet like pie,
Every slice prompts a happy sigh.
In this haven where jokes collide,
Nature's fun's our joyful guide.

Twilight Fragrance of Juicy Bliss

In the twilight glow, they sway and dance,
Chasing shadows while taking a chance.
Lemons laugh, and limes make a joke,
As oranges giggle, a ripe little poke.

With every twist, a zest-filled delight,
Citrus friends in the cool of the night.
Peeled laughter rains down, so playful and bright,
As the moon beams and echoes, oh what a sight!

Fruited Fantasies and Daylight

In the daylight sun, they plan their cheer,
Grapefruit grins with a wink and a leer.
Tangerines tumble, in playful spree,
While cherries roll on, full of glee.

Bananas slip as they join in the fun,
Singing sweet songs until day is done.
Peeling jokes like delightful rinds,
Fruits together, a bond that unwinds.

Chromatic Delight of Citrus Plots

In vibrant plots where colors collide,
Grapes and peaches take silly pride.
Watermelon types throw splashes of green,
While apples roll in, a fruity routine.

Pineapples twist with a gleeful flip,
Mixed fruit punch serves a laughter trip.
In the orchard's embrace, they laugh and shout,
With every bite, life's sweetness pours out.

Dappled Light on Amber Paths

Under the dappled light, they strut and play,
Fruits weaving warm tales on a sunny day.
Peaches prance while berries declare,
That citrusy jokes hang sweet in the air.

Kiwi confetti spills with flair,
While pumpkin and squash join the fair.
These golden paths lead to laughter's bloom,
In the heart of the grove, there's always room.

A Dance of Golden Spheres

In the grove they waltz and sway,
Orange balls brightening the day.
Laughter bounces from tree to tree,
As citrus fruits sing joyfully.

A squirrel joins in the fun,
Chasing shadows, on the run.
Slipping, sliding, oops, oh dear!
Where's your dignity, little deer?

Aromatic Harmony of Earth

Fragrant breeze, a playful tease,
Smelling sweet like honey bees.
Dance your way through zesty smells,
Where every fruit a story tells.

The beets are blushing, think they're fair,
But oranges have more flair to spare.
A fruit debate we must attend,
Who's juiciest? Let's not pretend!

Fields of Citrus Reverie

Fields of color, dappled bright,
Under sunshine, pure delight.
A pickle jumps, a tomato prances,
While tangerines take silly glances.

Lemons laugh with a zesty grin,
While grapefruits plot to wear a pin.
They joke of who will roll the best,
On sunny days they never rest.

Boughs Heavy with Sunlit Joy

Look up high, what do you see?
Branches laughing, wild and free.
A monkey swings with utmost glee,
Holding on tight, he's quite the spree!

A comet of color flashes near,
"Oh, what fun! Come join us here!"
With every bite the giggles swell,
In this fruity, fragrant spell!

The Dance of Twilight and Leaves

In the glow of twilight's gaze,
Leaves are twirling in a haze.
Branches creak with every sway,
Trees groove to end the day.

Squirrels waltz with little grace,
Chasing shadows, what a race!
Crickets chirp their nightly tunes,
While owls hoot at silly loons.

A breeze carries laughter near,
As peeking stars begin to cheer.
Every creature takes a chance,
In this twilight, all will dance.

Aromatic Journeys through Shaded Paths

Through leafy trails with scents so sweet,
Bumblebees sway on tiny feet.
Follow the whiskers of the breeze,
Into the realm of buzzing bees.

We stroll beneath the lemon sun,
Where our picnic is half the fun.
Ants march in a perfect line,
Seeking crumbs, how divine!

Paths adorned with scents galore,
Aromatic wonders at every door.
Yet slipping on moss, we giggle loud,
Falling down, we're feeling proud!

Radiant Fruits of Labor Past

Bright fruits hang like little charms,
Each one whispers of its farms.
With a wink, the lemons tease,
While oranges giggle in the breeze.

In baskets full of vibrant hues,
We sample flavors, what a snooze!
Marmalade plans go haywire too,
As we mix and stew, oh boo-hoo!

Sticky fingers, fruity bursts,
In our bellies, the joy still thirsts.
A treasure trove of tangy fun,
What a day—oh we've won!

Orchard's Lullaby to the Setting Sun

As the sun bows, trees hum soft,
Chirping birds fly high aloft.
Every leaf a joyful note,
In nature's band, we gladly float.

Mice play tag 'neath the boughs,
While sleepy squirrels take their bows.
A lullaby of rustles and sighs,
Beneath the canvas of painted skies.

Even shadows gather round,
For the sweetest dreams abound.
With every twinkle, eyes go dim,
In the orchard, we all swim!

Sunkissed Paradox of Sweetness

In a grove where bright fruits cling,
A squirrel critiques the joy of spring,
He hoards his treasures, oh so bold,
Deep down, he wishes he was sold.

A cat named Gus, with a curious meow,
Wanders through the trees, takes a bow,
Chasing shadows that tease and dance,
While he dreams of a juicy chance.

Bouncing bees with a goofy buzz,
They mistake the flowers for a fuzzy was,
Whirling round in a sunny daze,
Dancing like they're lost in a maze.

Laughter fills the air, a sweet parade,
While fruit-shaped hats start to invade,
In this silly world of zest and cheer,
Who knew the groves could bring such beer?

Nectarine Musings in the Grove

Beneath the branches, shadows sway,
Peelings on the ground decide to play,
A banana slips and yells with glee,
"Who left the fruit salad under the tree?"

The bees plan pranks with a buzzing song,
Plotting to steal apricots all day long,
While a wise old tortoise shuffles past,
At this party, time is unsurpassed.

Chickens chase the sun, a feathery race,
With carrot sticks as their delighting grace,
This farm-fresh frolic, how it tickles,
Comedy served with citrusicles.

Juggling lemons with a twist of fate,
A hungry chef tripped on a plate,
Dancing fruitcake, oh what a sight,
In this orchard, laughter's always bright.

Rustling Dreams of Amber Days

On amber days when sunlight gleams,
A duck with ambitions plots her dreams,
"Why swim alone when I can sashay?"
And quacks her way into a bouquet.

A mischievous wind swoops down to tease,
Leaves circle up like dandelion Frisbees,
In this tapestry of rustling fun,
Even the shadows have a punny run.

Pigs in shades lounge on grassy beds,
As thoughts of fruit pie dance in their heads,
With each giggle, an extra bounce,
How many oranges can one pig pounce?

This harvest tale, where giggles reign,
Finds joy in every little strain,
Under a sky so blissfully blue,
Where laughter ripens, and dreams come true.

Fragrant Secrets Beneath the Canopy

Beneath the green, a secret pact,
Is whispered by leaves, a citrus act,
A frog in shades sings a little song,
"Who knew the fruit could dance along?"

A wise old owl, with glasses tight,
Studies the happenings with delight,
"Is this a grove or a circus fair?"
Cuz circus nuts are flying everywhere!

A rogue raccoon steals a pomelo sweet,
Grinning wide as he munches his treat,
In a world where snacks grow on trees,
Even the critters can find their ease.

Jokes about jam spread far and wide,
As the sun dips low, spreading joy outside,
Under the canopy, laughter blooms,
In fragrant secrets of fun and fumes.

Echoes of Fruity Laughter

In a grove where citrus grows,
The trees are dancing, who knows?
One sneezed a fruit, oh what a mess,
Now the squirrels are in distress.

A jolly bee, buzzing near,
Sipping juice, spreading cheer.
Fruits giggle as they swing,
Each ripe laugh is a zesty thing.

Sunlight sparkles on each peel,
Every bite's a tasty reel.
Lemonade lakes, filled with screams,
Where everyone just loves their dreams.

The fruits conspire, what a plot!
A party planned, but forgot the cot.
Under their leaves, we hear delight,
A fruit fiesta, what a sight!

Vibrant Dreams Amongst the Trees

Amidst the branches, dreams take flight,
A ripe banana slid, oh what a sight!
With each twist and every spin,
The fruit parade is set to begin.

Apples chuckle with glee, oh dear,
Mangoes jive, no room for fear.
They paint the sky with joyful hues,
Hoping for just a splash of juice.

Plums share tales of their grand scheme,
In the glow, they plot and beam.
What fun it is to sway and prance,
These fruit-filled dreams lead to a dance.

In the shade, the laughter grows,
Cherry pies, not just for shows.
They throw a feast 'neath leafy beams,
In vibrant clumps of fruity dreams!

Juicy Secrets Hidden Beneath

Beneath the boughs, secrets creep,
Under the leaves, whispers leap.
Cherries giggle, hiding so well,
What juiciness do they have to tell?

Grapes gossip with a juicy flair,
Sipping nectar, beyond compare.
Hidden laughter in vibrant green,
Life here is a fruity scene.

On gentle breezes, jokes fly high,
Citrus orbs, oh me, oh my!
They tumble down, a playful bunch,
Prompting all to join the lunch.

Melons hatch a plot to tease,
Rolling around with so much ease.
They hold their secrets, oh so sweet,
Underneath where they all meet!

The Aroma of Sun-Kissed Blooms

In sunny glades, the scent divine,
With every breeze, the fruits align.
Petals bloomed, a fragrant spree,
Lemons and limes share their glee.

A whiff of laughter fills the air,
As giggling fruits spin everywhere.
Oranges wink, with zestful charm,
They beckon all to join the farm.

Jokes abound in every shade,
Scented whispers, no one's afraid.
Beneath the sun, the fruits unite,
In a floral comedy, pure delight.

With rays of gold all about,
The juicy tales, a joyous route.
Petals swirl in cheerful hues,
Aroma wraps around, like a fuse!

Citrus Dreams Underneath the Stars

Under the moon, the fruits all dance,
Branches sway, giving them a chance.
Squirrels giggle with citrus delight,
Peeled away from the mundane night.

Lemons wear hats, so bright and bold,
Tiny oranges boast stories untold.
Limes play tag, they run and they hide,
In this zesty world, we take a ride.

Juicy whispers float through the air,
As sweet as nectar, stripped of all care.
Stars twinkle down, laughing at dreams,
In this citrus realm, bursting at the seams.

Sipping moonlight in a glass so round,
With every sip, another giggle found.
Laughter rolls like thunder in the dark,
In the grove, we find our spark.

Whispering Leaves Tell Tales

Leaves rustle softly, sharing their schemes,
Puppies bark and chase their citrus dreams.
Branches gossip, twisting in the breeze,
Glimmers of laughter, dancing with ease.

A merry frog croaks jokes from his stone,
While bees buzz around, making honeycomb.
Ladybugs giggle at the silliest sights,
Fireflies twinkle, adding to the lights.

Every fruit holds a secret, so sweet,
Grapefruits whisper while the pigeons tweet.
In this green sanctuary, joy never slows,
Where each silly tale of nature grows.

Dancing shadows sway in the glow,
As laughter echoes fast and slow.
With every rustle, the stories unfold,
In this harvest of humor, let life be bold.

Nectar of a Sylvan Paradise

In a realm where juice rains down like dew,
Mice wear capes, swishing bright orange too.
A pineapple plays chess with a pear,
In this sweet garden, no one has a care.

Bouncing berries burst with color so bright,
As dancing kiwi twirls with pure delight.
In the bushes, giggles lighten the air,
This fruity fiesta beyond compare.

Caterpillars waltz with a rhythm divine,
Sipping sunshine like a good vintage wine.
With every chuckle, the branches sway wide,
In this paradise, we join in the ride.

Finally, a party behind every leaf,
Where laughter flows like a tap of relief.
Savoring nectar, sweet, luscious, and fine,
In this sylvan wonder, we sip, laugh, and shine.

Fruits of Memories and Time

Memories hang like fruit in the sun,
Each one giggles, reminiscing the fun.
Lost socks and tickles, all intertwined,
In the orchard of time, hilarity's kind.

Grapes share secrets about old vine sways,
Each twist and turn, a laugh that stays.
Bananas slip into jokes on repeat,
As cherries chuckle with a citrus beat.

In the harvest of laughter, we gather anew,
Swapping stories as the night slips through.
With every bite, the past comes alive,
In this fruity haven, our spirits thrive.

So toast to the fruits, and the memories spun,
In a landscape of laughter, where life is fun.
Each juicy tale, a sweet little rhyme,
In the fabric of laughter, the fruits of time.

Radiance of Ripe Fruits

In a grove of citrus cheer,
The fruits play hide and seek,
With laughter in the sunny air,
And squirrels that dance and sneak.

One orange rolled with glee,
Chasing shadows, what a game!
A lemon laughed, 'Come catch me!'
As they tumbled in their fame.

Beneath the trees, a picnic spread,
With zestful jokes and blissful bites,
A crowd of friends, all laughter fed,
Each bite erupts with fruity flights.

The juiciest tales were told,
Of sweetened dreams and fruity pranks,
In this garden, bold and gold,
Where every fruit gives thanks!

Honeyed Light Between the Leaves

In the dappled light, oh what a show,
A fig tried tangoing with a pear,
While cherries giggled, putting on a glow,
As bees buzzed in without a care.

Each leaf a stage, with joy to unfold,
The berries sang in tones so sweet,
Their notes of laughter never old,
With every sprinkle, they tapped their feet.

But one banana slipped and flopped,
'The fruit ballet turned slip and slide!'
While all around, the giggles popped,
As mangoes rolled, oh what a ride!

The nectar dripped like liquid fun,
A harvest filled with silly beats,
Beneath the sun, the games begun,
In this orchard, joy repeats!

A Symphony of Juicy Hues

In the morning light, so bright and clear,
A bouquet of fruits began to sing,
Oranges and grapes mixed with cheer,
As laughter danced on vibrant spring.

Lemons chimed in with zesty delight,
While limes rolled in with a twisty grin,
A harmony of colors, pure and bright,
As melons joined in, ready to begin.

A peach pranced lightly on its pit,
'Watch out!' it cried and took a leap,
As berries cheered, 'Don't you quit!'
While fruits juggled, their joy runs deep.

The symphony swelled with fruity dreams,
Each note a burst of golden fun,
Together they made the sweetest themes,
In this orchard, laughter spun!

Gardens Bathed in Amber

Beneath the sun's warm glow, so fine,
An apple dressed in stripes of bright,
Said, 'Join my feast, it's simply divine!'
As friends arrived, what sheer delight!

A comical cucumber slipped on juice,
And with a thud, it found its friends,
'Let's roll and dance, what's the excuse?'
As the laughter spilled with no end.

Every fruit adorned with silly hats,
Strawberries in shades of polka dots,
While cantaloupes shared giggly chats,
Their fruity fun connected the knots.

The festival bloomed, a fruity spree,
With games and jokes, oh what a sight,
In gardens aglow with energy,
Where laughter sparkled, pure delight!

Twilight Serenade in Orchard Isles

In the dusk, the fruit flies play,
Dancing on a bright orange display.
Lemons laugh, limes cheer;
It's a zesty party, let's all steer!

Grapefruits gossip under trees,
Talking about the latest breeze.
With zest and giggles all around,
Citrus jokes are quite profound!

Squirrels nibble while birds jest,
Who knew fruits could be the best?
An outburst of laughter, a juicy bite,
Twilight shimmers, oh what a sight!

As night wraps the orchard tight,
Citrus critters party till first light.
With mushy fruit and silly pranks,
They toast to laughter, with all their thanks.

Juicy Echoes of Summer's End

As summer waves its juicy goodbye,
Apples giggle, oranges laugh high.
Plucking fruit with a prankish hand,
A juicy wet slap – oh, how they planned!

Beneath a tree, a nap they take,
Lemons are dreaming of sour cake.
But one drowsy lime rolls straight down,
A citrus kaboom! A fruity clown!

The last harvest brings sprightly cheer,
Peanuts and fruit make a lovely beer.
Chillin' in the golden light,
They toast to flavors and silly sights.

As shadows stretch and night descends,
Citrus chuckles, the laughter bends.
Another season passed, oh dear,
Who's going to squeeze the fruit next year?

Golden Hues and Tangy Truths

In a grove where the sun does gleam,
Lemons debate who's the most supreme.
Tangerines chime in with a roar,
Bantering about fruit folklore!

Golden skin and tangy bites,
Fruits are dancing, what a sight!
Fuzzy peaches join in the feast,
Spinning in circles, they're the least!

Pecked by birds, squashed in a game,
Ripe jokes are traded, never the same.
A bee crashes, and chaos flies,
Sweet scents of laughter, oh my, what a rise!

As twilight signals the close of day,
Fruits smirk at the games they play.
Hiding their seeds, sharing the truth,
Silly stories of forgotten youth!

Blossoms and Breeze in Citrus Valleys

In valleys where blooms swing and sway,
Citrus blossoms plan their foray.
With a giggle and a springy pull,
They dance in circles, oh, how they lull!

A breeze whispers secrets, tickling leaves,
While fruits tell tales that one believes.
Nuts toss in laughter as they roll,
They're not just seeds; they're part of the whole!

Jovial oranges play peek-a-boo,
With cherries dressed in morning dew.
"Oh, what a fruity bunch we are!
Each bite's a giggle, each taste, a star!"

As the warmth wraps them snug and tight,
Fruits hold their laughter through the night.
In this valley, joy blooms and thrives,
Breezy whispers keep fun alive!

Harvest Celebrations in the Grove

In the grove, we dance and sing,
With oranges tossed like a ball,
A silly game, we catch the fling,
Laughter echoes, we're having a ball.

Juice stains on our shirts so bright,
Our faces smeared with zest and fun,
We trip and fall, what a sight!
Picking fruits 'til the day is done.

Those goofy hats worn askew,
As we juggle like circus pros,
Is it fruit or a fruit stew?
Who knows? The juiciness flows!

Later we feast, orange pie galore,
Citrus funny faces on every plate.
We toast to friendships, we want more,
In this fruity, funny fate!

The Language of Sun and Soil

Nature speaks in citrus tones,
With each sweet fruit, a giggle grows,
The sun winks down, the soil moans,
As we all trade our fruity woes.

Squirrels chatter, plotting schemes,
While bees buzz jokes, it seems absurd,
Trees sway to dance, follow their dreams,
As we listen to the orchard's word.

A worm in shades, a snail in flair,
They gossip secrets as we harvest,
"Oh dear, what's that?"—a cat in the air!
Guess a snack is the farmer's best.

So, let's toast with juice so bright,
Under the sun, we laugh and cheer,
For every blemish, brings delight,
In this jokester grove, year after year!

Golden Moments Beneath Fruit-laden Boughs

Beneath the boughs, we play and jest,
Golden treasures hang with glee,
Who knew fruits could be so blessed?
Silly faces—come climb with me!

Caught in a net, a fruit-fly chase,
'Round and 'round, we twirl with cheer,
Each landing spot, a warm embrace,
As laughter ripples far and near.

With baskets full, we strut and sway,
Pretending to be queens and kings,
With every slip, we shout, "Hooray!"
Who knew fruit could have such springs?

We'll paint our cheeks with juicy pride,
In this harvest, we'll forever stay,
The funny moments, side by side,
In golden afternoons of play!

Secrets of the Breezy Citrus Grove

In breezy groves where secrets hide,
The oranges whisper, "What's the fuss?"
With every breeze, they joke and glide,
"Oh dear, don't steal our juicy bus!"

A parrot squawks, "It's time to play!"
As squirrels wear hats; isn't that sweet?
They shimmy and shake in a fruity ballet,
Chasing after a rogue beet!

The sun winks at mischief we make,
While wind carries our laughter high,
We giggle, trip, and for fun's sake,
Pretend we're the clouds passing by.

So gather 'round for a feast so bright,
With wobbly fruits, we won't fit in,
For in this grove, we feel just right,
With breezy laughter, we always win!

Sunlit Boughs of Citrus Delight

In sunlit boughs, the fruits hang high,
With juicy tales that make us sigh.
A squirrel dances, slips on a peel,
While giggling birds give quite the squeal.

Bees buzz loudly, wearing their crown,
On nectar nectar, they're never down.
A butterfly, with wings that glint,
Pours orange juice—oh, what a hint!

Neighbors gather, a taste test spree,
With faces sticky, oh my, whee!
One bites hard, and juice flies wide,
What a show, come join the ride!

Laughter spills from the garden fair,
Citrus whispers fill the air.
With every twist, a giggle bursts,
In sunlit boughs, we quench our thirst!

Zestful Whispers Among the Leaves

Zestful whispers among the trees,
The wind plays tricks, gives quite a tease.
A plump fruit wobbles like a clumsy dance,
And down it drops—oh, what a chance!

The cat sprawls out, it snores up high,
While lizards dart, low and spry.
They're racing fast, in silly ways,
Who knew leaves could be such a maze?

Lemonade drips from chins so wide,
Kids giggle, splash, and slip with pride.
A clumsy aunt takes a tumble too,
Landing soft, with zest on her shoe!

Amid the laughter, we lose all cares,
With every fruit, surprise declares.
Beneath the sun, where fun's the goal,
The orchard whispers, marbles roll!

Harvest Moon over Hanging Fruit

Under the harvest moon's soft glow,
Hanging fruits put on a show.
A raccoon dons a little hat,
Sings a tune, plump and fat!

Buckets full, but wait, oh no,
Someone's slipping, to and fro.
A juicy bounty, ripe and sweet,
Turns an outing to a retreat!

Around the tree, the friends convene,
With goofy smiles, their faces gleam.
A challenge to catch a fruit on a head,
Brings laughter loud, and then they spread!

With every toss, a giggle's made,
Scenarios funny, never fade.
Moonlit joy, with fruit in sight,
We cherish the fun, all through the night!

Citrus Dreams in Dappled Light

Citrus dreams in dappled glow,
Fruity visions dance below.
A ladybug, in polka dot dress,
Bids the orange to impress!

It rolls away, she chases fast,
Her tiny legs are built to last.
While laughter rings through every nook,
As tiny worlds a twist will cook!

Juicy tales of the citrus gang,
A woeful lime, who lost its tang.
Orange jokes fly through the air,
Tickling all—does anyone care?

In shady spots, the laughter swells,
With zesty quirks, the story tells.
Where every fruit, ripe with cheer,
Creates the sweetest joy we hear!

Tantalizing Treasures of the Earth

In a grove where fruit hangs low,
Laden branches sway to and fro,
I met a thief with a sly grin,
He offered me one, I let him in.

He claimed it's gold, a true delight,
But took one bite, what a fright!
A squirt of juice flew, oh what fun,
Turns out he's just a clumsy one.

With every laugh, the trees would sway,
As friends joined in, they laughed away,
Tantalizing, yes, but what a mess,
Splat on the ground, true happiness!

Citrusy chaos, bright and bold,
A world of wonders, stories told,
Nature's gags, oh sweet surprise,
In fruity jokes, joy truly lies.

Glimmering Dreams of Zesty Bliss

A silly thought of drinks so bright,
I mixed some zest, it felt so right,
But who would sip this yellow brew?
I think I'll pass, how 'bout you?

With a wink and twist, I tried anew,
A fizzy splash! Oh, where it flew!
The neighbors laughed, they rolled in glee,
My drink exploded, oh mercy me!

Each drop that lands adds to the fun,
Sparkle and giggles, we just run,
A potion sweet, with a hint of chaos,
Our fruity party, quite the pathos!

Dreams that glimmer, laughter so grand,
In the mirthful rush, we took a stand,
Zesty bliss, we toast with cheer,
Raise a glass, let's spread some here!

Nature's Palette in Sunset Hues

As dusk arrives with a painted scene,
Palettes burst with colors so keen,
A farmer tripped, oh what a sight,
His bucket flipped, a colorful flight!

A swirl of orange, purple, and green,
Nature's joke, especially mean,
The dogs rolled in, so frisky and bold,
Drenched in hues, a sight to behold!

Flowers laughed and trees would sway,
Birds chirped songs in a lively play,
Sunset giggles, oh what a tease,
Each stroke of color, nature's ease!

In jests of balance, mishaps sung,
We danced, we laughed, the night was young,
Painting joy in every hue,
Masterpieces that felt brand new!

A Legacy of Sweet and Sour

Gather round for tales to tell,
Of citrus fruits that ring a bell,
Sweetness dancing, oh what a tease,
Sours too bold, but bring you to knees!

I tasted tales of joy and pain,
A tarty bite, like summer rain,
Fruits of laughter, a shove and shout,
A legacy that leaves no doubt!

Grandma's recipe calls for zest,
But mix it wrong, you'll fail the test,
Sour surprises in every bite,
We chuckle and cry, what a delight!

A family feast, both sweet and bold,
Stories shared, and memories fold,
A juicy chuckle, a snappy roar,
In every taste, a bit of folklore.

Dreaming in Citrus Colors

In a grove where laughter grows,
Chasing shadows, where the sun glows,
Lemons giggle, oranges dance,
Fruitful jokes in citrus pants.

Bees in bow ties, buzzing away,
Tickling petals in a sunray,
Branches sway, a comedic show,
Citrus clowns put on a glow.

Squeeze those cheeks, make a face,
Vitamin C at a fun pace,
Jellybeans dressed in zestful skin,
Jumping high for the fruity win!

A squirrel jokes with a cheeky grin,
As juicy fruit does a silly spin,
Citrus dreams, let's take a ride,
In this orchard, joy won't hide.

The Serenity of Fruit Laden Branches

High above, the branches sway,
Orange globes in bright display,
Birds in hats take to the skies,
Chirping puns with funny ties.

Sipping sunshine, fruit cocktails,
With giggles and squeaks, life prevails,
Leaves rustle, sharing a jest,
It's a fruit festival, oh what a quest!

Bouncing fruit and a bouncing mood,
Dancing bees in a citrus brood,
Even the shadows wear a grin,
In this haven, laughter's a win.

Tasting sweetness, a fair delight,
As we twirl in zesty flight,
So let's clink our cups with glee,
To the joy of fruit-filled spree!

Whispers of Citrus Tales Untold

Underneath the leafy spout,
Fruits conspire, laugh and shout,
Oranges tell their timeless tales,
While grapefruits wear colorful veils.

Twirling lemons, sprightly spritz,
Sharing secrets, silly bits,
Lime jokes float on a fruity breeze,
Chuckles rise among the trees.

A sour face? Not in this place,
As oranges race in a juicy chase,
Citrus chortles, sweet and bright,
Echo through the afternoon light.

Grapes rolling, what a sight,
Peeling laughter, pure delight,
So gather 'round, let's sip away,
In this orchard, fun leads the way!

The Allure of Summer's Richness

In the sunlight, a treasure found,
Golden fruits all around,
A merry band on a juice-filled quest,
Making lemonade, we're surely blessed.

Melons burst with a hearty cheer,
While citrus fools bring us near,
Orange hats and lemon shoes,
Wobbling tunes and sweet fruit blues.

Pies flying through the air with glee,
Cheeky squirrels plotting a spree,
Sticky fingers from juicy bites,
Laughing 'til the summer nights.

Breathe it in, this juicy air,
Citrus giggles everywhere,
Let's gather round for one last shout,
In this fruitful fun, there's no doubt!

Ripe Lullabies in the Wind

In the grove where fruit does sing,
A squirrel juggles, what a thing!
He drops a ball, then slips and falls,
Laughter echoes through the walls.

Buzzy bees in a dance parade,
Searching blooms for the sweet cascade.
They bump and fumble, then buzz and flee,
A buzzing ballet in glee and spree.

Underneath the lemon tree's shade,
A cat naps, unafraid,
While mice sneak by, in tiny shoes,
They tiptoe past, not making news.

With branches heavy and sun so bright,
The shadows play, a merry sight.
A toad jumps high, then lands with a sigh,
The grove's a circus, oh me, oh my!

Sunlit Bounty's Gentle Call

Stranger fruits hang from branches wide,
A dragonfly takes a joyride.
It zips and zooms, then runs out of gas,
Plops down in zest, then rolls on the grass.

A pig in boots starts a waltz near,
With twirls and snorts, it's hard to peer.
The laughter swells like a juicy roar,
As the pig pretends it's a dancing floor.

Grapefruit drops with a mighty thud,
Catapulted by a rolling bud.
It's frisbee time in this sunny land,
As friends chase fruit; what a funny band!

Lemons giggle, their skins gleam bright,
While critters race with sheer delight.
In this jewel, where oddities reign,
Happiness flows like a juicy vein!

Rustling Secrets of the Grove

In a shady nook, a rabbit hops,
With floppy ears that never stops.
He hears a joke from a friendly bee,
And snickers lightly by the tree.

A sleepy owl with glasses on,
Reads stories to the leaves at dawn.
They rustle 'round, excited to hear,
As punchlines pop and giggles near.

Under oranges, where shadows crouch,
A turtle thinks it's time to slouch.
He takes a nap on a cozy mat,
While ants parade by in a line, quite fat.

With whispers soft and chatter clear,
The grove is alive, full of cheer.
Secrets shared in the sun's embrace,
In this funny, leafy place!

Morning Dew Amongst Citrus Dreams

The morning dew like jewels shine,
On leaves that shimmer, oh so fine.
A curious crow starts to tease,
Squeaking jokes to the buzzing bees.

A wise old tortoise in a race,
Moves so slow, it's quite the pace.
With a shrug and grin, he claims his prize,
"Winners, just those with sleepy eyes!"

Oranges giggle in the breeze,
While critters sway like dancing trees.
A caterpillar makes a shout,
As Karoke star, truly stands out!

In these dreams where antics bloom,
Hilarity fills every nook and room.
Nature laughs, no worries on the seam,
As everyone basks in citrus dream.

Serenade of Citrus Spheres

In a grove so bright and round,
Lemons giggle on the ground.
Oranges bounce in merry cheer,
While limes just roll without a fear.

Grapefruits challenge every tree,
"Pick me first!" Oh, what a spree!
Citrus fruits wear cheerful hats,
Dancing 'round like playful cats.

Tangerines joke as they sway,
"Who's the juiciest?" they play.
With zest they tease the summer sun,
Creating laughs as they just run.

When the harvest day draws near,
Squirrels laugh with fruit-filled cheer.
Oh, the joy upon the bough,
Nature's joke, just take a bow!

Fields of Alluring Citrus Whimsy

In fields so bright with colors bold,
Citrus tales are oft retold.
A lemon wears a silly grin,
While orange pops, it's such a win!

The tangerines put on a show,
They twist and jump, delighting so.
A grapefruit hums a quirky tune,
While limes just bounce beneath the moon.

With wagging leaves, they play charades,
A fruit parade that never fades.
The sun beams down, it joins the fun,
As laughter grows, it's never done.

In this land of juicy jest,
Each citrus fruit feels quite blessed.
With every laugh and fruity cheer,
These fields bring joy, it's crystal clear!

Where Sun Meets the Earth's Embrace

Beneath the bright and blushing sun,
Citrus fruits just aim to run.
Their peels are bright, their smiles wide,
In sunshine's glow, they laugh with pride.

With every breeze that tickles leaves,
The citrus globe just takes a squeeze.
Lemonade flows from comical boughs,
Despite the bees, they laugh and vow.

Oh, how they play in grassy nooks,
With sunshine popping in the crooks.
A fruit feud starts, and oh, the fun,
Who will dance until day is done?

Not a worry in the orchard's song,
They twirl and giggle all day long.
With zest for life, they take their place,
In nature's sweet and funny space!

Nature's Sweet Haven

In this haven where fruits collide,
Grapefruits grin and oranges glide.
With every laugh, the breeze goes wild,
A citrus ruckus, bright and styled.

The lemons crack a zesty joke,
While tangerines tease with a poke.
A playful battle of fruity glee,
Shade beneath leaves? A sight to see!

A fruit ball game begins in the sun,
"Catch me, catch me!" Oh, what fun!
Juicy dribbles all around,
With laughter echoing abound.

In nature's nook, they all convene,
A sweet utopia, fresh and keen.
With every twist and citrus rhyme,
They find their joy in sunny clime.

A Tapestry of Citrus Skies

In a grove where fruits do dance,
A cheeky squirrel takes a chance.
He flips and flops, so wild and spry,
While I just watch, and let out a sigh.

The lemons giggle, lemons glow,
They tell me secrets, quite a show.
The tangy tales of morning cheer,
Turn my frown into a beer.

The branches sway, in playful jest,
A sunbeam tickles, it's truly best.
The oranges pop, like joke on cue,
And I'm just here, sipping fruit brew.

So grab your sunhat, come on down,
Join the fruit parade, wear your crown.
With laughter ringing, life's a treat,
In citrus lands where antics greet.

Echoes of the Sweetly Pruned

In a garden where the trees are neat,
Chickens cluck with dainty feet.
They peck at dreams and cackle loud,
As if they're the coolest in the crowd.

A lemon's cut, and laughter's fried,
The juice escapes, I'm taken for a ride.
With every squirt, a silly fight,
Who knew that zest could spark delight?

Around the trunks, a dance parade,
Juggling fruits, a grand charade.
The oranges roll, the apples cheer,
While I just stand and sip my beer.

The sun dips down, the shadows play,
Bouncing off the fruit ballet.
Let's toast to prunes, and squeeze some fun,
In this wacky grove, we're all just one.

Luminous Orbs on Silken Branches

In a canopy where laughter sways,
The shining orbs have funky ways.
They bounce and tease with zestful glee,
Be careful—don't get sticky, flee!

With whispers sweet, the fruits conspire,
Launching seeds like tiny fire.
Radar squirrels chase after dreams,
In this orchard, folly beams.

The petals flutter, a fashion show,
Where dandelions steal the glow.
With citrus crowns and snickers loud,
We prance around, so fruitfully proud.

The twilight comes, the stars ignite,
We giggle at the sheer delight.
In the branches, stories loop,
As laughter hangs, the fruity troupe.

Footprints in Amber Light

In hues of gold, the sun drip-drops,
While cheeky raccoons dance on tops.
They slide and flip, a furry race,
Leaving footprints, a silly trace.

The tangerines whisper, "Come and play,"
While zucchinis join in the fray.
With every twist, a crunch is heard,
We've started the loudest fruit third!

From branches high, fruits dare to swing,
Creating chaos, oh what a fling!
The lemons laugh with pulp-filled pride,
As I trip over, but I won't hide.

Now the day fades in amber light,
Citrus giggles fill the night.
In this wild patch of pure delight,
Let's dance till dawn, it feels so right.

www.ingramcontent.com/pod-product-compliance
Lightning Source LLC
Chambersburg PA
CBHW070310120526
44590CB00017B/2617